Change It!

Solids, liquids, gases and you

Written by **Adrienne Mason**
Illustrated by **Claudia Dávila**

Kids Can Press

Kids Can Press acknowledges the financial support of the Government of Ontario, through the Ontario Media Development Corporation's Ontario Book Initiative; the Ontario Arts Council; the Canada Council for the Arts; and the Government of Canada, through the CBF, for our publishing activity.

Published in Canada by
Kids Can Press Ltd.
25 Dockside Drive
Toronto, ON M5A 0B5

Published in the U.S. by
Kids Can Press Ltd.
2250 Military Road
Tonawanda, NY 14150

www.kidscanpress.com

The artwork in this book was rendered in Photoshop.
The text is set in Century Gothic.

Series editor: Valerie Wyatt
Edited by Christine McClymont
Designed by Julia Naimska
Science consultant: Jean Bullard

The hardcover edition of this book is smyth sewn casebound.
The paperback edition of this book is limp sewn with a drawn-on cover.
Manufactured in Tseung Kwan O, NT Hong Kong, China, in 3/2016 by Paramount Printing Co. Ltd.

CM 06 0 9 8 7 6 5 4 3 2
CM PA 06 20 19 18 17 16 15 14 13 12 11

Library and Archives Canada Cataloguing in Publication

Mason, Adrienne
     Change it! : solids, liquids, gases and you / written by Adrienne
Mason ; illustrated by Claudia Dávila.

(Primary physical science)
Includes index.
ISBN 978-1-55337-837-2 (bound)
ISBN 978-1-55337-838-9 (pbk.)

1. Matter — Properties — Juvenile literature. I. Dávila, Claudia
II. Title. III. Series.

QC173.36.M34 2006   j530.4   C2005-907024-2

Kids Can Press is a *l'orus*™ Entertainment company

Contents

Matter around you

Matter is all around you. You are matter, a toy boat is matter and water is matter. Matter is anything that takes up space. Matter can be a solid, a liquid or a gas.

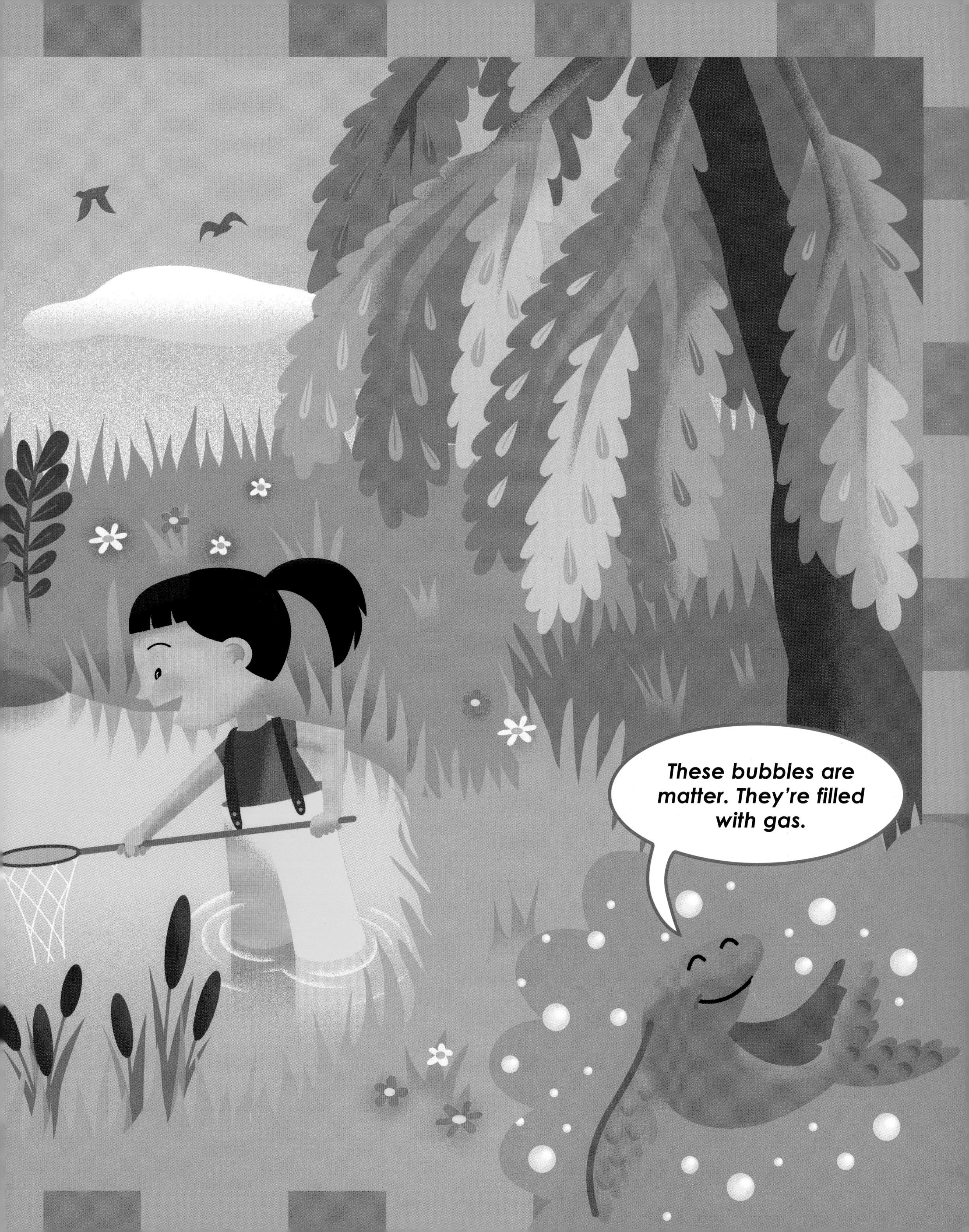
These bubbles are matter. They're filled with gas.

What's a solid?

Solids have their own shape. Rocks are solids. Hats and skipping ropes are solids, too. Solids don't change shape easily. You can stretch a skipping rope, but when you let it go it takes its own shape again.

Can you find three more solid objects in the picture?

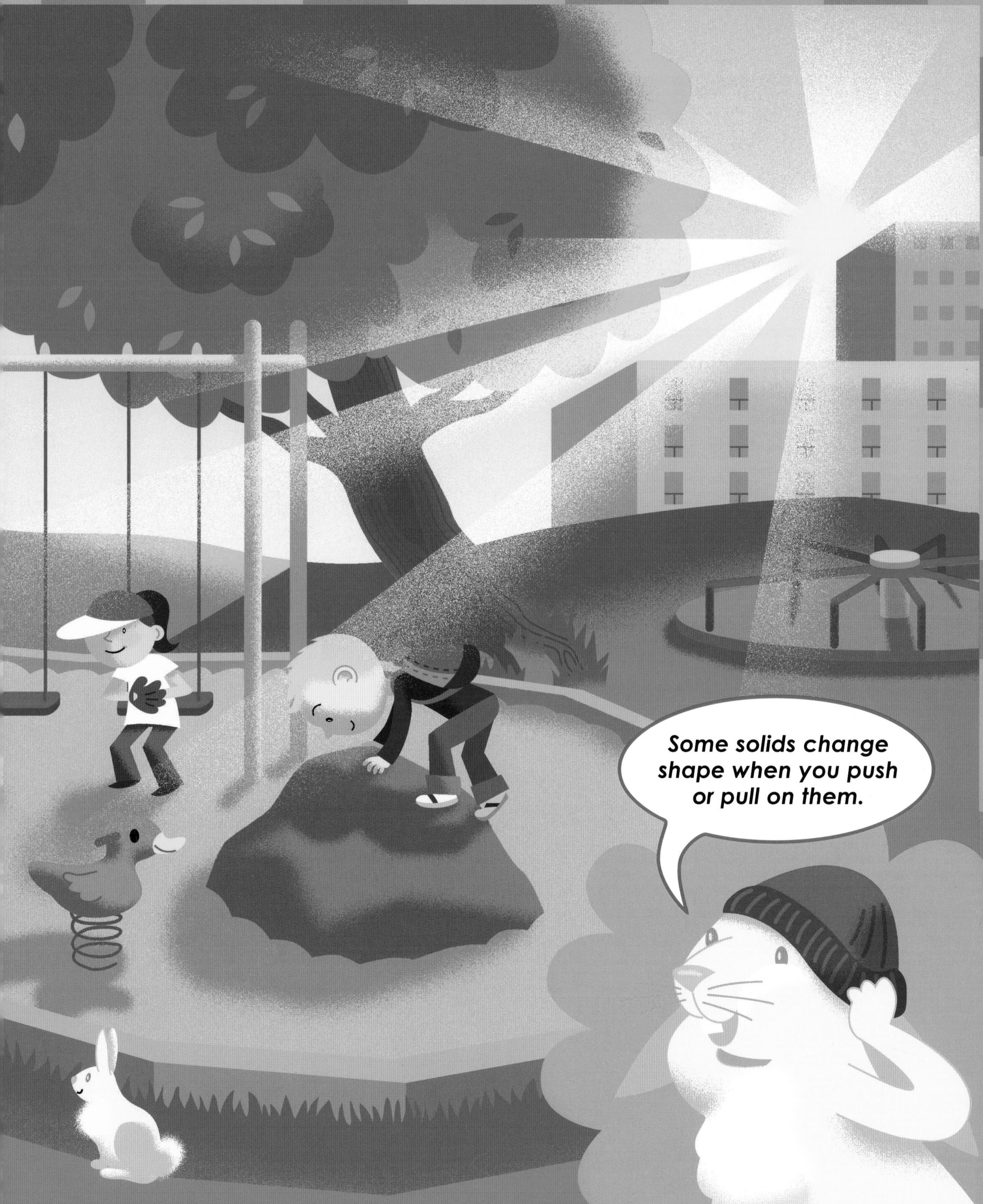
Some solids change shape when you push or pull on them.

Change its shape!

Play dough is a kind of solid. If you change its shape, is it still a solid? Make some and see.

You will need

- 250 mL (1 cup) flour
- 60 mL (1/4 cup) salt
- a mixing bowl
- a spoon
- 125 mL (1/2 cup) hot tap water
- food coloring

What to do

1 Mix the flour and salt in the bowl.

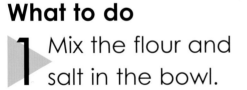

2 Have an adult add the hot water. Stir well.

3 Use your hands to knead the dough. If it is too sticky, add a sprinkle of flour.

5 Use the dough to make different shapes. Store leftover dough in a plastic container in the fridge.

4 Add the food coloring and knead for 5 minutes.

What's happening?

The play dough keeps the shape you mold it into. Solids keep their shape unless you do something to change them.

I changed the shape of this chocolate bar, but both parts are still solid.

What's a liquid?

A liquid has no shape of its own. Liquids change shape easily. Liquids also flow. When you pour a liquid into a container, it takes the shape of the container — a glass, a bottle or a bucket.

How many liquids can you find in this picture?

Pour it in!

Can your friend guess which container holds more liquid? Find out.

You will need

- a measuring cup
- water
- 3 empty clear plastic or glass containers of different sizes and shapes
- food coloring

What to do

1 When your friend isn't watching, pour 250 mL (1 cup) of water into each container.

2 Add two drops of food coloring to each container.

3 Ask your friend to guess which container holds the most water.

4 Pour the water from the container your friend chose back into the measuring cup. Show her how much water was in the container.

5 Now pour the water from the other containers into the measuring cup, one at a time. Your friend will see that each container was holding the same amount of liquid.

What's happening?

Liquids take the shape of their containers. The amount of liquid can look greater or smaller depending on the container.

Uh-oh! This container is too small.

What's a gas?

Gas is all around you, even if you can't see it. The air you breathe in and blow out is a gas. A gas has no shape of its own. Gases spread out to fill their container — a bubble, a bicycle tire or even a room.

14

Fill it up!

Can you fill a balloon without blowing air into it?
Try this.

You will need

- a balloon
- a small funnel
- a teaspoon
- baking soda
- vinegar
- a juice or pop bottle

What to do

1 Stretch the neck of the balloon.

2 Put the funnel into the neck of the balloon.
Add two large spoonfuls of baking soda to the balloon.

16

3 Pour vinegar into the bottle. Stop when it is half full.

4 Ask an adult to help you with this step. Stretch the neck of the balloon over the opening of the bottle.

5 Hold the balloon upright. Let the baking soda fall into the vinegar.

What's happening?

When you combine baking soda and vinegar, they make a gas. This gas spreads out to fill the bottle and then the balloon.

The fizz in my pop comes from tiny bubbles of gas.

Freezing and melting

Solids can change into liquids when they warm up. When a solid snowflake lands on your warm tongue, it melts and changes into liquid water.

Liquids can change into solids when they cool down. Because it's cold out, the water in this pond has frozen into ice.

Cool it!

How can liquids and solids combine to make ice cream? Try this to find out.

You will need

- 250 mL (1 cup) whole milk (a liquid)
- 5 mL (1 teaspoon) vanilla (a liquid)
- 15 mL (1 tablespoon) sugar (a solid)
- 1 small sealable plastic bag
- 1 large sealable plastic bag
- 12 ice cubes (solids)
- 30 mL (2 tablespoons) salt (a solid)

What to do

1 Put the milk, vanilla and sugar into the small plastic bag. Seal the bag well.

2 Place the ice cubes in the large plastic bag. Sprinkle the salt on the ice.

3 Place the small bag in the large bag. Seal the large bag well.

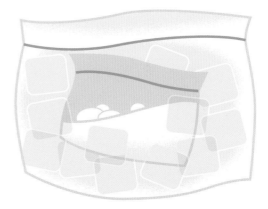

4 Put on some music and shake the bag for 10 minutes.

5 Scoop your ice cream into a bowl and enjoy.

What's happening?
The ice cools the milk and sugar. Then this liquid mixture changes into a solid — ice cream.

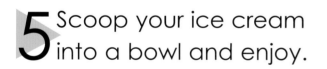

I'd better eat my ice cream fast before it melts into a liquid.

Wonderful water

After it rains, there are puddles. But puddles soon dry up. The warmth of the sun makes liquid water change into a gas. This gas is called "water vapor."

Water can be a liquid, a solid or a gas. Can you find all three in this picture?

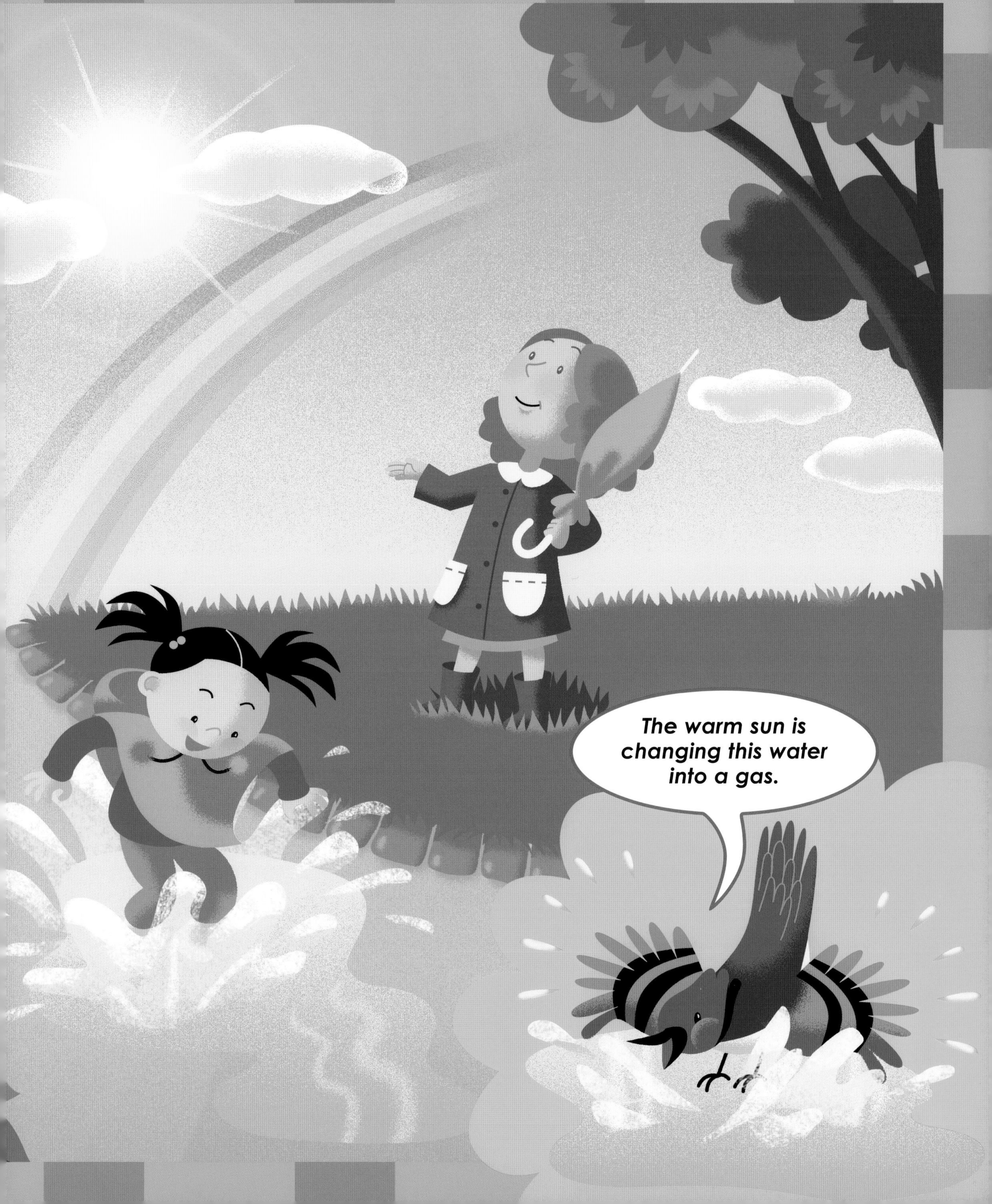
The warm sun is changing this water into a gas.

Paint with salt!

How can you make a picture by painting with salty water? Try this to find out.

You will need

- 60 mL (1/4 cup) warm water
- a small plastic or glass container
- 30 mL (2 tablespoons) Epsom salts
- a paintbrush
- 1 piece dark construction paper

What to do

1 Pour the warm water into the container. Add the salt. Use the paintbrush to mix the salt in the water.

2 With the paintbrush, paint a simple picture on the construction paper.

3 Let the paper dry. What do you see? Where did the water go?

What's happening?

The warm water disappears because it changes into water vapor. The salt, a solid, stays on the paper and makes your picture.

High in the sky, water vapor cools down and turns into clouds.

Mixing matter

You can combine solids and liquids to make something new. When you bake a cake, you mix together eggs and milk (liquids) with flour, sugar and butter (solids). When you put the mixture into a hot oven, gas bubbles form. This gas makes the batter rise so you get a fluffy cake.

Solids, liquids and gases

Matter is anything that takes up space. Matter can be a solid, a liquid or a gas.

Solids don't change shape easily. They have to be pushed or pulled, heated or cooled.

Liquids can flow. They take the shape of the container they are in.

Gases have no shape. They spread out to fill the space they are in.

For parents and teachers

The information and activities in this book are designed to introduce children to solids, liquids and gases. Here are some ways you can help them explore the concepts further.

Matter around you, pages 4–5

Every living and nonliving thing is made of matter. Matter has mass and takes up space. Children will be able to understand the idea that matter is something they can see, feel or smell. There are three main states of matter: solids, liquids and gases. Ask children to identify and describe matter in the illustration and in the world around them. In the picture, the solids include the tree, boat, people and flowers. The liquid is the water in the pond. The gas is the air all around, and inside the bubbles in the pond.

What's a solid?, pages 6–7

Solids have a definite mass and shape. Typical "hard" solids include metal, rocks, wood and ice. Solid matter keeps its shape unless an outside force acts upon it. A great deal of force (a push or a pull) is needed to change some solids. Other solids can change shape more easily, when only a small amount of force is applied. Collect a variety of solids for children to examine; for example, a crayon, paper clip, sponge, ribbon and cookie. Take children on a walk to look for more solids, both indoors and out.

Change its shape!, pages 8–9

Solids keep their shape unless they are pushed or pulled. Play dough is a solid whose shape can be easily changed. When children work with play dough in this activity, they can see that it holds the shape they mold it into. Talk about other ways children could change the shape of solids. For example, they can break a crayon, cut a ribbon or crumble a cookie. As with play dough, these smaller pieces hold their shape and remain solid matter.

What's a liquid? and Pour it in!, pages 10–13

Liquid matter can flow. Let children experiment with a variety of liquids such as milk, liquid honey, molasses and juice. Assemble different sizes and shapes of containers. Pour the liquids from one container into another to demonstrate how they flow. For example, honey flows more slowly than milk. (Some solids, such as dry macaroni or jelly beans, can also "flow," but these small solids do not change shape after they are poured.)

What's a gas?, pages 14–15

A gas is matter that has no shape of its own. Gases spread out and fill whatever container they are in. Gases can be difficult for children to visualize. Show that they can feel a gas (moving air) when the wind blows or when they blow on their hand. To demonstrate how gases spread out to fill whatever space or container they are in, open a bag of freshly popped microwave popcorn in a room. The warm gas rising from the popcorn will fill the room. In the picture, the smell of the loaf of bread is spread by gases.

Fill it up!, pages 16–17
The balloon blows up because the gas spreads out to fill the container — the balloon. Gas pushing on the walls of the balloon inflates it. The gas produced in this reaction is carbon dioxide.

Freezing and melting and Cool it!, pages 18–21
Solids and liquids can change state when they are cooled or heated. Show children some examples, such as freezing juice to make frozen treats, or melting chocolate or butter by setting it in a sunny window. Butter and chocolate will both become solid again when they are cooled in the refrigerator.

Wonderful water, pages 22–23
Water is the only substance that is found in nature as a solid, a liquid and a gas. On pages 18–19, the children saw what happens when water freezes and becomes a solid (ice). Here, they see how water can evaporate (change from a liquid to a gas).

Tell children that water can also change from a gas (water vapor) to a liquid when cooled. This is called condensation. The clouds in the picture form when water vapor cools and condenses into water droplets in the cloud.

Paint with salt!, pages 24–25
This activity demonstrates the effects of evaporation. When the water evaporates, it becomes water vapor (a gas) and leaves the salt (a solid) on the paper. Talk about other examples of evaporation, such as a wet bathing suit drying on a warm summer day.

Mixing matter, pages 26–27
Water can freeze and melt and freeze again without becoming a new kind of matter. Sometimes, however, when you change a state of matter, the process can't be reversed. In this activity, solids and liquids are mixed and then baked. The resulting solid is a different type of matter — a cake. The change is irreversible. Ask the children what happens when you cook (heat) an egg. Can this change be reversed?

Solids, liquids and gases, pages 28–29
Have children cut out pictures of the three states of matter from magazines. Make a wall chart with three columns: Solids, Liquids and Gases. Have children place their pictures in one of the three columns. For the gas column, they can show the effect of a gas; for example, a kite or flag blowing in the wind.

Words to know

gas: matter that spreads to fill the space it is in

liquid: matter that flows and takes the shape of the container it is in

matter: any substance — solid, liquid or gas — that takes up space

solid: matter that holds its own shape

Index